The First Irish In Illinois: Reminiscent Of Old Kaskaskia Days

Patrick T. Barry

In the interest of creating a more extensive selection of rare historical book reprints, we have chosen to reproduce this title even though it may possibly have occasional imperfections such as missing and blurred pages, missing text, poor pictures, markings, dark backgrounds and other reproduction issues beyond our control. Because this work is culturally important, we have made it available as a part of our commitment to protecting, preserving and promoting the world's literature. Thank you for your understanding.

Jeremiah Curtin

THE FIRST IRISH IN ILLINOIS

REMINISCENT OF OLD KASKASKIA DAYS

BEFORE THE ILLINOIS STATE HISTORICAL SOCIETY
AT ITS THIRD ANNUAL CONVENTION AT
JACKSONVILLE, JANUARY 23
AND 24, 1902

BY P. T. BARRY

CHICAGO NEWSPAPER UNION
NEWSPAPER AND MAGAZINE PRINTERS
CHICAGO

*Mr. Jeremiah Curtin,
with regards of
the writer.
P. T. Barry.*

Harvard College Library
Sept. 3, 1913
Bequest of
Jeremiah Curtin

PREFACE.

At the kind invitation of some of the officers of the Illinois State Historical Society, this paper was written.

It was an afterthought on my part to have it published in this little brochure, thinking that in this form those who may not have the leisure to go through many researches for the information here gleaned, might like to learn something of the important part taken by the Irish element in the exploring, settling and development of the great West.

We of Irish birth and lineage should endeavor to get our proper place in the history of the country's achievements. At every stage of its eventful history, whether in the peaceful conquests of its trackless forests and prairies to civilization, or on land and sea in the assertion and defense of its liberty and integrity, the Irish element have stood shoulder to shoulder with others of their fellow-citizens in the good work.

It is not only a pardonable pride but a praiseworthy duty on our part to rescue from oblivion and have compiled into history for the truthful information of posterity the noble deeds of our ancestors, whether as pioneers, explorers or patriots, in this great American republic of ours.
P. T. BARRY.

THE FIRST IRISH IN ILLINOIS

Individual Irishmen appeared early on the scene in Illinois. They came in a military capacity. Having no government of their own to serve, they served others. The Irishman who had the distinction of first figuring in our annals was a Chevalier Macarty, who succeeded LaBussoniere in 1751, in the command of the first French fortress erected in the Mississippi valley—that of Chartres. He came from New Orleans with a small military force, and remained in charge until 1764, when he delivered up that stronghold to the English, according to the treaty of 1763, by which France yielded up all her Canadian possessions by right of conquest to her ancient enemy.

Canada at that time extended to the Ohio River on the south and to the Mississippi on the west. There was not yet any map bearing the name of the Empire State of the West. There was only a tribe of Indians inhabiting a portion of the immense Northwest named the "Illini," that had its name given to the territory at the dividing up. Beyond the Mississippi was Spanish territory.

Under the French and Spanish systems of colonization at that date, Indian missions, military posts and towns went together. Old Kaskaskia, in what is now Randolph County, was the first seat of civilization in the great Mississippi basin, and was for a time the capital of the Territory. Here many stirring events took place for many eventful years. In addition to a mission and a fort near by, it was made of greater importance with a legislature. Pere Marquette, the apostle of several States, laid its foundation in the year 1675, one hundred years before the breaking out of the war for American independence. Here savages and whites commingled. Also, the soldiers of France, Great Britain and America. And wherever there are soldiers there is to be found the ubiquitous Irishman. There was to be found

French contentment, savage resentment and pioneer endurance. Vincennes, Pittsburg and Detroit were its nearest neighbors on the great Western expanse. But, like the sites of Tyre and Sidon, famous in ancient history, it exists no more, the encroaching waters of the Mississippi having washed it away and made it a memory.

After the capitulation of Quebec in 1763 the British claimed ownership of the whole of the French territory known as Canada, and prepared to garrison all the forts the French had erected, including Detroit, Peoria, Vincennes, Chartres, Cahokia, Kaskaskia, etc. The last-named three were situated on the Mississippi River, and somewhat contiguous.

On the 27th day of February, 1764, a Major Loftus of the British army, then on duty in Florida, was ordered to proceed to Fort Chartres and take possession of it. His name indicates his Irish origin, but if there be any mistake in this, there certainly was not in his soldiers. They were of the Twenty-second British regiment, and were mostly Irishmen. Here, then, was presented the peculiar spectacle of one Irish commander in the service of a country not his own being required to evacuate his command to another Irishman in the service of a different country not his own. It reminds the writer somewhat of the Siege of Quebec by Richard Montgomery, an Irishman in the service of the United States, when he asked its British commander, Sir Guy Carleton, another Irishman, and an old schoolmate, to surrender to the Continental Congress. But Major Loftus was not fortunate any more than General Montgomery. On the way, he and his command were attacked by the Indians, killing many of the soldiers, the remainder escaping down the Mississippi. Thus was the first Irish blood spilled in the Mississippi valley.

Then another Irish officer, also in the British service, named George Croghan, was ordered by Governor Murray to go forward and secure the desired possession. Croghan had been quite a conspicuous figure in the British interest in those days in America. He ranked as Major, and had been for many years a trader among the Western Indians. Hardly another white man was in the prairie country before him. In describing the country afterwards, he said it looked like an ocean. The ground was exceedingly rich and full of all kinds of game, and at any time, in half an hour, he could kill all he wanted. He was commanded to go from Fort Pitt to make the way clear for the British advance to Forts Cahokia and Chartres. It was not the French alone that were to be considered, but the Indian Chieftains, as well. He first sent forward a Lieutenant Fraser to see the way clear, but the latter received rough treatment at Kaskaskia and returned unsuccessful. It was said that Chief Pontiac was egged on to kill him, but he escaped without serious injury. Then Col. Croghan, who was also a British Deputy Superintendent of Indian Affairs, went forward himself. He left Fort Pitt (now Pittsburg) on May 15, 1765, accompanied by a party of friendly Indians. His progress was uninterrupted until he arrived at a small promontory on the Wabash, where he disembarked. On June 8, six miles below the stream he was suddenly attacked by a band of Kickapoos, eighty in number. In the fight which followed Croghan lost two white men and three Indians, while most of his party, including himself, were wounded. A surrender was unavoidable, and the victorious Kickapoos plundered the entire party. Subsequently the Indians confessed they had made a great mistake, and expressed sorrow for what had happened. They supposed, they said, that the friendly Indians accompanying Croghan were their deadly enemies, the Cherokees. They brought their prisoners in safety to Vincennes on the Wabash, where the Indians, many of whom had friendly acquaintance with Croghan, strongly condemned the Kickapoos, and the latter in turn expressed deep sorrow for what they persisted in calling a blunder. Further on the way he received a message from St. Ange, the late French commander, cordially inviting him to advance to Fort Chartres. He had proceeded but a short distance on his way, however, when he was met by a delegation of chiefs, representing various tribes of Indians, among whom was the hitherto implacable Pontiac, the great warrior, at the head of a large band of Ottawa braves, offering their services as an escort. At this juncture, and under this condition of things, Croghan did not deem it necessary to proceed further in person. the British claim to the territory being acknowledged by both French and Indians. This happy state showed that the Irishman must have used his diplomatic powers to excellent advantage. He then betook himself to Detroit to attend to other important business in the interest of his royal master, leaving his command in charge of another officer.

Accompanied by Pontiac Croghan crossed to Ft. Miami and descending the Miami held conferences with the different tribes dwelling in the immense forests which sheltered the banks of the stream. Passing thence up the Detroit he arrived at the fort on the 17th of August, where he found a vast concourse of neighboring tribes. The fear of punishment and the long privations they had suffered from the suspension of their trade had banished every thought of hostility, and all were anxious for peace and its attendant blessings. After numerous interviews with the different tribes in the old town hall where Pontiac first essayed the execution of his treachery, Croghan called a final meeting on the 27th of August. Imitating the forest eloquence with which he had long been familiar, he thus addressed the convention:

"Children, we are very glad to see so many of you present at your ancient council fire, which has been neglected for some time past. Since then high winds have blown and raised heavy clouds over your country. I now, by this belt rekindle your ancient fires and throw dry wood upon them that the blaze may ascend to Heaven, so that all nations may see it and know that you live in peace with your fathers the English. By this belt I disperse all the black clouds from over your heads that the sun may shine clear on your women and children, and that those unborn may enjoy the blessings of this general peace, now so happily settled between your fathers the English and you and all your younger brethren toward the sunsetting."

PONTIAC'S REPLY.

"Father, we have all smoked together out of this peace pipe and as the great Spirit has brought us together for good, I declare to all the nations that I have made peace with the English In the presence of all the tribes now assembled I take the King of England for my father and dedicate this to his use that henceforth we may visit him and smoke together in peace."

The object of Croghan's visit being thus accomplished he was prepared to depart, but before doing so he exacted a promise from Pontiac that the following spring he would appear at Oswego and enter into a treaty with Sir William Johnson in behalf of the Western nations associated with him in the late war.

In September, 1768, came John Wilkins, Lieutenant Colonel of "His Majesty's Eighteenth or Royal Regiment of Ireland," and commandant throughout the Illinois country. Several companies of this regiment came with him from Philadelphia and occupied quarters at Kaskaskia. The experience of those troops was not good, but it was common to that of all new comers in the aguish "American Bottom." The sickness among them was not only very great, but very fatal. At one time, out of five companies, only a corporal and six men were found fit for duty.

Captain Hugh Lord became the next commander of the Royal Irish Regiment, and continued so until the year 1775. The British Governor at Kaskaskia at this time was a Chevalier Rocheblave, strange to say a Frenchman. It was at this time that the Colonists began to defy George III., and the Irish soldiers of the old French outposts were persistent in showing sympathy for them, and their leaning toward the American cause was such that poor old Rocheblave declared it worried him to see men of British birth giving him more trouble than the French. After a time most of the Irish soldiers of Britain were drawn off for service elsewhere, and the French residents were organized into militia. Their Captain was one Richard McCarty, a resident of Cahokia. There was another McCarty who built a water mill on the Cahokia creek near Illinoistown at a later date, who was known as "English McCarty."

In 1777, Irish Americans began to appear on the scene, with the invasion of General George Rogers Clark, the Virginian. What Clark's ancestry was remains in some doubt. His biographer, English, thinks his ancestors came from Albion, but is able to give no particuuars. The Scotch-Irish Society claims that he is of Ulster blood. At any rate he conquered that portion of British territory that had formerly belonged to the French, and from which five sovereign States of the Union have been carved. His army was composed of Virginians and Pennsylvanians, many of whom were Irish either by birth or by blood. He was materially assisted by the French settlers, under the leadership of Father Gibault, the republican priest of Kaskaskia. To the latter and one Col. Francis Vigo, a native of Sardinia, who was married to an Irish lady (a Miss Shannon) was the success of the Virginian invasion mostly due, and the annexation of the prairie country to American territory. Clark affiliated very closely with the Irish. It is due to him to say that he was a brave and generous man, whose services to his young country can never be forgotten. His invasion of this wilderness and its conquest, it must be remembered, was under the direction of Governor Patrick Henry of Virginia, and to him alone he was responsible. The first of his Irish relatives to deserve notice was William Croghan, a nephew of Major George Croghan, the British officer already alluded to. He cherished no love in his heart for Great Britain or her monarch. He had resigned the British for the American service. He left Ireland for America when quite young, and was long in the employ of the British as an Indian agent, like his uncle. He joined the American forces at Pittsburg and witnessed the surrender of Cornwallis at Yorktown. He married Lucy Clark Rogers, sister of the famous general. When he joined the American forces, he was assigned to Col. Werder's Virginia regiment, shortly after the battle of Long Island, and continued in active service for years. He was promoted to the rank of Major in 1778, and was assigned to Col.

John Neville's Fourth Virginia regiment and participated in the battle of Monmouth. He marched with the Virginia troops to Charleston, South Carolina, where the whole American army at that place was compelled to surrender to the enemy. In 1781 he was paroled and went to Virginia with his friend, Col. Jonathan Clark, brother of the general, and for a time was the guest of Col. Clark's father in Caroline County. It was there he met the woman who was destined to be his wife. He was afterwards a delegate to the Kentucky convention of 1789-90, and was one of the commissioners to divide the land allotted to the soldiers engaged in the conquest of the Northwest. He left six sons and two daughters. One of his daughters became the wife of Thomas Jessup, Adjutant-General U. S. A. His son George married a Miss Livingston, of the noted New York family. This son George greatly distinguished himself at the battle of Tippecanoe in 1811, and subsequently in the Mexican war. He was a Major at the time of his defense of Fort Stephenson at Lower Sandusky, and Congress presented him with a medal for his gallantry. A splendid monument has been erected to his memory at Fremont, Ohio. The elder Croghan died in 1822, and his widow in 1838.

Francis Eleanor Clark, youngest daughter of the old hero, married Dr. James O'Fallon, whom the memoir says was a finely educated Irishman who came to America shortly before the revolution. He was an officer during the war for independence, and was the founder of the well-known O'Fallon family of St. Louis, and which has been so conspicuous in the history of that great city. There is also a town named after one of the members of this family in St. Clair County, this State. To his two grandsons, John and Benjamin O'Fallon, General Clark willed 3,000 acres of land.

Another nephew and heir of the General, was George Rogers Clark Sullivan, who was honorably identified with Indiana affairs during the territorial period, and who left a long line of prominent descendants, after one of which is named Sullivan County in that State.

In General George Rogers Clark's army for the conquest of Kaskaskia, Cahokia and Vincennes were many men with Irish names, and when we take into account the Irish, then so very numerous in Pennsylvania and Virginia, it would not be surprising if one-half of it was composed of Irishmen and Irish-Americans. In this army were 236 privates, besides officers. Some of the names of the latter are as follows: Major Thomas Quirk (who was originally a sergeant in Captain McHarrod's company and rendered some military service on the frontier before and after the Illinois campaign). Clark's biographer says "Quirk was a brave and fine-looking Irishman." He died in Louisville, Kentucky, in the fall of 1803. He was allotted 4,312 acres of land for his valuable army services.

Captain John Montgomery, who is stated in one place to be "an Irishman full of fight," was one of Clark's most valued officers, and had been one of the celebrated party of "Long Hunters."

Col. John Campbell, who was one of the commissioners for the allotment of Clark's land grant of 149,000 acres, to the men engaged in his Illinois campaigns, was an Irishman by birth, and a man accredited with much force of character. He was a member of the Kentucky convention of 1792, and a member of the legislature. He died without issue. After Campbell came James F. Moore, Alex. Breckenridge, Richard Taylor and Robert Breckenridge, as land commissioners. James F. Moore had been a soldier under Clark, and also, subsequently, a member of the Kentucky House of Representatives. Here are names that are suggestive of subsequent presidents of the United States. Richard Taylor was a native of Virginia, of Irish extraction. He removed in 1785 to Kentucky; was a soldier of the revolution holding the rank of Lieut.-Col. at its close. He was the father of the hero of the Rio Grande, Gen. Zachary Taylor, and twelfth President of the United States. Robert Breckenridge, also of Irish extraction, was a member of the Kentucky Legislature, and Speaker of the House of Representatives several times. He was the ancestor of John C. Breckenridge, Vice-President with

THE FIRST IRISH IN ILLINOIS.

James Buchanan, and subsequently a presidential candidate himself.

Col. Archibald Lochrey was County Lieutenant of Westmoreland County, Pennsylvania, and started with his command from Carnahan's block-house August, 1781, to join Gen. Clark's Illinois forces, with a company of volunteer riflemen raised by Capt. Robert Orr; two companies of Rangers under Capt. Thomas Stockley, and a company of horse under Capt. William Campbell, for the reduction of Detroit, then in the possession of the British. Stockley was met and defeated by Indians in the British service. In fact, the whole of Col. Lochrey's expedition was defeated, forty-one men being killed, and the rest taken prisoners. When certain facts with regard to the British forces became known at Kaskaskia, it was determined to raise a small American force and make a raid against Fort St. Joseph, a British post situated on the St. Joseph River. The company consisted of only seventeen men and was commanded by Thomas Brady, a patriotic Irish-American citizen of Cahokia, who had emigrated hither from Pennsylvania, and who was described as being "both restless and daring." He marched across the country in October and succeeded in eluding the Indian guards and capturing the place, taking a few British prisoners, together with a large quantity of goods. Being over-confident, on his return he was attacked by a force of Pottawattomies and British traders, hastily organized for the purpose, and while laying encamped on the Calumet River, near Chicago, was defeated. Two of his men were killed, two wounded, and ten taken prisoners. Brady, with two others, succeeded in making their escape, and returned to Cahokia. But he did not rest until he organized another expedition to rescue his friends and avenge his defeat. He was joined by a party of Spaniards from the west side of the Mississippi, then Spanish territory, and retook the place without striking a blow, and the Spanish flag for a short time replaced the British. The event was a small one, but Spain had the cheek to demand the country on account of it.

This Thomas Brady, and one William Arundel (an Irishman

from Canada, and an Indian trader in Cahokia in 1783) and Capt. Richard McCarty, already mentioned, and a small party of hunters that joined General Clark's expedition in 1778, were the only white men in Illinois territory besides the French Canadians, and a few old soldiers, at the time of Clark's conquest. They resided at Cahokia. Brady was afterwards Sheriff of St. Clair County.

Among other names of officers that are likely to have been Irish or Irish-American in Clark's army, are those of Col. Benjamin Logan, Capt. John Baily, Capt. Robert Orr, Capt. William Campbell, Col. William Davis, Lieut. Martin Carney, Thomas Dalton and Major Denny.

General Clark wrote a letter to the Governor of Virginia (Patrick Henry) from Kentucky on October 12, 1782, in which he said, "I had the pleasure of receiving your letter by Major Walls and Mr. Kearney, the 30th of July past, at which time the gentlemen arrived with stores all safe, after surmounting uncommon difficulties. They arrived in time to save troops from deserting." This shows that the Irish were pretty well in evidence both in Virginia and the Northwest at that period.

Subjoined is a list of the privates taken from one page only of the printed roster of Clark's soldiers of the Illinois expedition, that were entitled to receive, each, 108 acres of land, as printed in English's life of General Clark: Moses Lunsford, Abraham Lusado, Richard Luttrell, John Lyons, Joseph Lyne, Francis McDermott, David McDonald, John McGar, Alex. McIntyre, Geo. McMannus Sr., John McMannus Jr., Samuel McMullen, James McNutt, Florence Mahoney, Jonas Manifee, Patrick Marr, Charles Martin, Nathaniel Mersham, Abraham Miller, John Montgomery, James Monroe, John Moore, Thos. Moore, John Murphy and Edward Murray.

James Curry was the name of one of Clark's soldiers who proved himself a rather extraordinary fellow, and a fearless pioneer. A band of Indians had wounded a comrade of his named Levi Teel, in his own house, when Curry was present. Seeing the enemy coming he jumped up into the loft of the house, with the hope of driving them away before Teel could have time to open the door to admit them. He shot three times and killed an Indian every time. He then got down to see what had happened to Teel, and found him transfixed by one of his hands with a spear to the floor. Curry got up again into the loft and tumbled the whole roof down, weight-poles and all, on the Indians, who were standing at the door with spears in their hands. Their chief was killed, and the others ran away. Curry hurried to Kaskaskia for help, and at last saved himself and companions from death. He was at the capture of Fort Gage and Sackville, the names given by the British to the old French forts. Curry was a great athlete, contending in all sorts of games, and was not unlike Thomas Higgins, another great Irish Indian fighter of a later date. In all desperate and hazardous services, Clark chose him, first of all, to act in places of peril and danger. Curry and Joseph Anderson, who afterwards lived and died on Nine Mile Creek, Randolph County, were out hunting, and the Indians, it is supposed, killed Curry, as he went out from their camp and never returned. This was the sad end of one of our bravest and most patriotic Irish-American heroes, "the noble-hearted James Curry," as he is styled in history, and whose services were so conspicuous in the conquest of Illinois. His body was never recovered.

Edward Bulger was a private in Capt. Joseph Bowman's company in the Illinois campaign. He was afterwards an ensign in Captain William Harrod's expedition against Vincennes, and in General Clark's first expedition against the Indians in Ohio. He was mortally wounded in the battle of Blue Licks, 1782, at which time he had been promoted to the rank of Major. He was one of the early explorers of Kentucky, where he was with Hite, Bowman and others in the spring of 1775. These were probably the first white visitors to what subsequently became Warren County. Hugh Lynch was another of this party, and William Buchanan another. Daniel Murray was the name of an Irishman who supplied provisions for Clark's Illinois army.

One of the forgotten names of men who did great service to the republic in the revolutionary war was Oliver Pollock, an Irishman born. He performed the same kind of service in the West that Robert Morris performed in the East. He financed General Clark's military campaign in Illinois and Indiana, and without his aid they must have been failures. He was born in Ireland in the year 1737 and came to America with his father. On account of his intimacy with General O'Reilly, who was then Governor of Cuba, he was able to borrow from the royal treasury of Spain the sum of $70,000, which he lent to the State of Virginia for Clark's use in the campaigns mentioned. He was not reimbursed, and consequently was not able to make good what he had borrowed, which caused his arrest and imprisonment in Havana. He died in Mississippi in 1823.

In 1777, when Clark was approaching Kaskaskia to surprise the British, then in possession of the fort, he took two men from that party of American hunters led by one John Duff, that he met on the way, to act as his spies. They had left Kaskaskia but a few days before. These men were Jas. Moore and Thomas Dunn, as to whose nationality, from their names, there can be no mistake.

General St. Clair, a Scotsman, was afterwards military commander of the Northwest. He was succeeded by General Anthony (Mad Anthony) Wayne, an Irishman born, who conducted the war with the Indians in 1791. Under St. Clair the battle of Ft. Henry was fought and resulted in a great American disaster. But General Wayne gained a great victory at the Maumee Rapids on August 20, 1794, which led to the suspension of hostilities.

One of the authorities that we have recourse to in writing these annals is the "Pioneer History of Illinois," by ex-Governor John Reynolds, a man of Irish parentage, born in Pennsylvania, and who filled nearly every office, legislative, judicial and administrative in the State of Illinois. His place of residence was Cahokia, a short distance north of St. Louis, on the Illinois side.

John Reynolds, in his "Pioneer Days," described his father as "an Irishman who hated England with a ten-horse power," and there is no surmise in saying that he himself hated her just as much, as he was an ardent admirer of "Old Hickory." Neither did he want to be set down as an Anglo-Saxon. He repulsed the insinuation in the following emphatic language:

"Our old enemies, the English, and their American friends, give us the name of New Anglo-Saxons. It is true the most of the Americans are the descendants of Europeans, but the preponderance of blood is not of the Anglo-Saxon race. There are more of the descendants of the Irish and Germans in the United States than the English." If that were true seventy years ago, certainly it is more true now.

We have already alluded, in connection with Curry's achievements as an Indian fighter, to the name of Tom Higgins. One of his noted encounters with Indians, is described in Governor Reynolds' book, with thrilling effect. This noted Irish-American pioneer resided in Fayette County for many years, where he raised a large family, and died in 1829. He received a pension, pursued farming, and at one time was doorkeeper of the General Assembly at Vandalia.

John Edgar was a merchant at Kaskaskia, and at that time the richest man in the territory. His wife was a lady of rare talents, and presided over the finest and most hospitable mansion in Kaskaskia. At this house was entertained General LaFayette, when he visited this country in 1825. Mr. Edgar's memory is honored by having an Illinois county named for him.

In Mrs. Robert Morrison, Kaskaskia possessed another lady of Irish ancestry, who was an ornament to Illinois society at that early day. Mrs. Morrison was reared and educated in the City of Baltimore, and in 1805 she accompanied her brother, Col. Donaldson, to St. Louis; then in the far-off wilds of the West, whither he was sent as a commissioner to investigate the title lands. She was married the following year to Robert Morrison of Kaskaskia, which place became her residence thereafter. Well educated, sprightly and energetic, she possessed a mind gifted with originality, imagination and romance. Her delight was in the rosy field of poetry. Her pen was seldom idle. She composed with a ready facility and her writings possessed a high degree of merit. Her contributions to the scientific publications of

Mr. Welch of Philadelphia, and other periodicals of the period, in both verse and prose, were much admired. Nor did the political discussions of her day escape her ready pen. She was a member of the Roman Catholic Communion, and shed lustre on her co-religionists. The Morrison family is one of the best known politically and socially in the State. While Mrs. Edgar entertained Gen. LaFayette at a grand reception, Mrs. Morrison entertained him with a grand ball on the occasion referred to in the foregoing.

The territory of Illinois was organized on the 16th day of June, 1809. Michael Jones and E. Backus were appointed respectively registrar and receiver of the land office in Kaskaskia. At this time one McCawley, an Irishman, had penetrated further into the interior of the territory than anyone else—to the crossing of the Little Wabash by the Vincennes road.

The writer cannot resist the temptation to relate an anecdote of General James Shields, a hero of the Mexican war, who cut so conspicuous a figure in old Kaskaskia days. The anecdote he related himself, in a lecture delivered in Chicago shortly before his death. He arrived in Illinois on foot soon after he left Ireland for America, looking for employment. On the way, he fell in with a young man engaged in a similar pursuit, and who was companionable, so they traveled together. Reaching Kaskaskia, Mr. Shields secured employment there, as a school teacher, and remained. His companion was not so successful, and went on, traveling in the direction of St. Louis. Shields rapidly rose from one position of distinction to another, and when the Mexican war was declared he was filling the position of a land commissioner at Washington. He hastened to Kaskaskia with President Polk's commission in his pocket, to raise an Illinois regiment, of which he was to be Colonel. He was successful in this, went to Mexico, and distinguished himself in several battles, in one of which he was supposed to be mortally wounded, but recovered. He became a General and a hero. When the war was over and he returned to the United States he was lionized and invited to a number of State fairs and cities as an attraction. St. Louis honored him in this way, and made unusual preparations for his reception. The Mayor and corporation went out to receive him. His reception was most cordial. The Mayor grasped him warmly by the hand and looked him significantly in the face. "Do you not know me, General?" he asked. "I do not, Mr. Mayor, who are you?" "I am the man who tramped with you to Kaskaskia, many years ago, and walked on to St. Louis."

"Good God! I am delighted to see you," was the exclamation of his distinguished guest.

The Irish not only made history in those early days, but have also written it. To the pen of John B. Dillon of Indiana, we are indebted for the best history of the Northwest; to John Gillmary Shea of New York we are under obligation for a complete knowledge of the early Catholic missions among the Indians, and ex-Governor Reynolds has narrated for us our own pioneer story, with its grotesque conditions, its many deprivations and numerous deeds of daring. For many of the incidents in this essay, especially those relating to General George Rogers Clark and his men, and the conquest of the Northwest, I am indebted to the "Life of General Clark," by a Mr. English of Indiana.

Were it not for the fear of making this essay too long, I might show how fifteen to twenty names of Illinois counties have Irish associations; what prominent parts Irishmen and the sons of Irishmen of Illinois took in the war of 1812, the Blackhawk war, the Mexican war and the war of the rebellion; how they filled gubernatorial chairs, prominent positions in State and nation, as the representatives of the people; how they have been foremost in the professions of law, medicine and divinity. On the muster roll of famous men they have three Logans, the two Reynolds, Carlin, Kinney, Ford, Kane, Shields, Ewing, McLaughlin, Mulligan, Medill, Ryan, and many others too numerous to mention. Not as public and professional men alone has the Irish contingent been valuable to the State of Illinois, but also as tillers of the soil, as miners and manufacturers; for in the infantile condition of our commonwealth the men of hardest muscle and most exacting toil were our Irish immigrants. They did the excavating on our canals, and the grading on our first railroads, and wherever hard work was to be performed, there you were sure to find Paddy with his spade and pipe. May I not claim that that herculean form representing "the Digger," in the statue of Mulligan, standing at the entrance of the Drainage Canal, near Chicago, answers for the Irish canaler of former as well as later days?

Nearly fifty years ago Thomas D'Arcy McGee, an American Irish poet, and at the time of his death a leading statesman of Canada, of wide fame and renowned memory, wrote of the Irish prairie farmer in Illinois as follows:

> " 'Tis ten long years since Eileen bawn
>   Adventured with her Irish boy
> Across the seas and settled on
>   A prairie farm in Illinois.
>
> "Sweet waves the sea of Summer flowers
>   Around our wayside cot so coy,
> Where Eileen sings away the hours
>   That light my task in Illinois.
>
>   Chorus—
> "The Irish homes of Illinois,
> The happy homes of Illinois,
>   No landlord there
>   Can cause despair,
> Nor blight our fields in Illinois!"

Printed by Libri Plureos GmbH in Hamburg, Germany